KINDLE UNLIMITED

Everything You Should Know Before Subscribing...Or Not

Mark Sheppard

Disclaimer and Terms of Use: Effort has been made to ensure that the information in this book is accurate and complete. However, the author and the publisher do not warrant the accuracy of the information, text, and graphics contained within the book due to the rapidly changing nature of science, research, known and unknown facts and internet. The Author and the publisher do not hold any responsibility for errors, omissions or contrary interpretation of the subject matter herein. This book is presented solely for motivational and informational purposes

ISBN: 978-1981587209

Printed in the United States

MAPLEWOOD
– PUBLISHING –

Contents

Is Kindle Unlimited The Subscription Service For You?

My finger wanted to hit the button. My mind warned it to stop dead in its fingerprints. "You'll be sorry," my mind told the finger. There, poised above the "send" button on Amazon.com, my index finger hovered.

I was deciding if the Kindle Unlimited subscription plan was as good a deal as the program claimed it was. And if it were, was it the right plan for my reading habits? If I pushed this button I had, at my fingertips, access to every book Kindle placed in the program for a mere $9.99 a month.

Before I committed myself to even a 30-day free trial, it would be wise, my brain continued, to do more research.

That, in a nutshell, is how this publication was born.

So I did all the research I could find in order to make an intelligent decision. Once all the material was stored in my jump drive, it seemed like a logical extension to write it all down. That way, other individuals, wondering the same things I had, could at least benefit from my research.

The Self-Crowned King of Publishing

It's no secret that in the past several years, Amazon has not only found a niche in the publishing industry but has also turned the business on its head. Kindle Unlimited is only one of a list of innovations which it introduced to readers and to traditional publishers and authors who prefer what's now being called, "self-publish." Even a partial list of the revolutionary ways this giant has transformed the landscape of the book business is impressive:

- Low-cost print books
- Kindle E-Book Reader
- Easy self-publishing
- Lending Library as part of Amazon Prime
- Encouraging self-publishing

These few changes have struck at the heart of the publishing industry like nothing since the advent of desktop publishing. Kindle Unlimited is merely the latest in this list. I'm here to help you navigate this latest innovation in reading convenience. Before your mind allows your finger to push that button, you should know exactly what you're getting into.

Among the items covered in this publication that will help guide you through your own decision-making process are:

- An overview of the program
- The differences between Kindle Unlimited and other subscription ebook programs
- Getting the most mileage out of your 30-day free trial
- Discovering participating books
- Learning if it's the right subscription program for your reading habits
- Learning the difference between the benefits of Kindle Unlimited and Amazon Prime membership
- How to cancel your membership
- What happens to the books you've already downloaded
- The effects the program has on self-publishers, traditional publishers and authors.
- And much more!

Don't hit that button for even a free trial until you've learned more about the program. This publication offers you an impartial look at Kindle Unlimited. Based on this – at times eye-opening – information, then you'll be able to decide whether it's worth your "reading time" to join.

Not only that, but this book also covers how Kindle Unlimited affects those who earn at least part of their income through publishing. How do they feel about the program? And how do they get compensated for their work?

This book wasn't made to either discredit the Kindle Unlimited subscription service or serve as a mouthpiece for Amazon. Instead, it was written to help give you a scorecard of what you'll be getting for your monthly fee. It was also written to help you take a good look at your reading habits – and your attachment to "owning" books – among other criteria, to help you decide if the plan is right for you.

In the next section, you'll be cutting through the "hype" of the program – all the sugar-coated benefits – as described by its proponents, to what you're actually receiving for your monthly fee.

It's all here, so grab your favorite beverage and chair, and read all about it!

Kindle Unlimited: Beyond the Hype

Kindle Unlimited is what's known as a monthly ebook subscription service. You, as an avid reader, pay the monthly fee of $9.99 and are given unlimited access to some 700,000 books in their electronic form, and another 2,000 audio books. These books can be downloaded to your Kindle or any device of your choosing which has a Kindle application installed in it.

It's easy enough to find these books on Amazon. Any book that's included in the program is clearly marked as part of the Kindle Unlimited program as shown in the image above.

Simply click on the "kindleunlimted" logo beneath the price of the book. To the right of the logo it directs you to "read this book for free."

Finding the Unlimited Books on Your Kindle

It's even easier to search for participating books from your Kindle. There are two ways to do this. The first is to simply turn on your reading device, and click on to the area marked "Kindle Unlimited." This will provide you with a listing of the books from which you can choose.

If you're looking to read a specific nonfiction topic or genre, enter that into your Kindle or app. You'll get a listing of those books. Below the title and author of the book, it'll indicate if it's part of the subscription service.

If you've missed this labeling, then when you click to specific book, the Kindle Unlimited program logo appears immediately below the "buy" button. In fact, if you're a member of the service, the logo is already lit. All you have to do is to click the "read for free" button search for it as you do with any book through your ereader. Once you click, you'll only have seconds to wait before it's in your menu and available to read.

Misconceptions from the Start

You might be tempted to think that your $9.99 a month allows you to "buy" these electronic books. No. And you may believe that the name of the program, "Kindle Unlimited" allows to go crazy clicking away on every book you've wanted to read. You'd be wrong on both counts.

8

When Amazon encourages you "read this book for free," that's exactly what they mean. As a member, you'll click and the book will be delivered to your Kindle or app just as if you would have bought it, through the magic of technology, in this case labeled "Whispersync" by Amazon.

The giant bookseller allows members to download a total of ten titles to every account at one time. Once you've reached your ten-book limit, you can't get another until you've returned one of the ten in your reading device. At that point, once you've "returned" a book, you then can replace it with another.

You'll probably enjoy your membership more knowing that it's really a form of a lending library for electronic books more than the old-fashioned "book of the month club."

Returning a Book

Returning a Kindle Unlimited book is easy enough. If you're on the Kindle device yourself, you simply go to the Kindle Store and navigate to the program's landing page by selecting the tab "all categories" and then choosing the Unlimited tag. It's here you'll find the return button. Simply hit that and as quickly as the book appeared on your device, it will "disappear."

You return an Unlimited book from any app in a similar manner. You'll go to the area marked "Manage your content and devices." From the section marked "Your Content," you use the various menus to navigate to the Kindle Unlimited section and then the "books" portion.

After you select "Actions," you simply choose "Return the Book," and the book is swept off your computer.

Once you return a book and you have less than the maximum ten books in your device through Kindle Unlimited, you'll be allowed to download another.

Amazon Prime versus Kindle Unlimited

If the Kindle Unlimited program sounds vaguely familiar, you might already be an Amazon Prime member. The drawing card to that program is the free shipping. As part of the program, though, you have access to what the site calls the "lending library."

This service allows anyone who holds a Prime membership to borrow an ebook as part of the paid service. The difference between this and the Unlimited service is that members can only borrow a single book at a time. Once that book has been returned, they can then borrow another. Another difference of the two services is that with the Prime membership, borrowed books can only be read on Kindle devices and not on the reading applications.

In the initial stages of the Kindle Unlimited plan, it was only available in the United States. As the service expanded over the years, its availability has also expanded. Amazon is constantly updating that list. If you're wondering if it's available in a specific country, it would be best to check it out on its website.

The Pros and Cons of Kindle Unlimited for the Reader

If you're an avid reader, this subscription service seems like a no-brainer, especially if you're already a regular customer of Amazon. How can you tell if Kindle Unlimited is worth the monthly fee? Check this list of characteristics. If even a few of these traits describe you, then you'd probably be quite satisfied with a membership.

Advantages

1. **You're a voracious reader.**

Face it, you love to read. Not only does it seems as if you can't get enough of novels, you're an avid reader of nonfiction as well. Chances are great you'll find ten books – the upper limit of downloading – in a matter of minutes and read through these in no time.

Many lovers of romance novels would be in this category. There are also devotees out there of fantasy and science fiction books. These readers simply cannot satisfy their reading appetite.

2. Looking for new authors and genres relatively risk free?

Then this program works for you. For $9.99 a month, you can explore those new authors you've been hearing about from friends, family, and various web sites. This certainly is better than spending twice that amount on one book, only to find the author's style or story doesn't appeal to you.

3. You don't even need a Kindle to take advantage of the service.

That's right! If you don't happen to have a Kindle, you can still take advantage of this service through the use of any Kindle application for just about any electronic device. If you want to read from your tablet, there's a Kindle app for that. Similarly, do you want to read from your smart phone? Yes, there's an app for that. Even more exciting than being able to down load the app is downloading the app for free.

You really should give this fact some thought, especially if you are already a member of prime. The Amazon lending library attached to that service doesn't extend to Kindle applications. You can only use it on proper Kindle devices.

4. If your current budget for books can't handle your appetite, then Kindle Unlimited is just what you need.

Many individuals love to read. And they'll sit down and read . . . and read . . . read. If this sounds like you, then you'll probably get use out of your monthly subscription fee for the program – and more.

This is especially true with those in the romance and cozy mystery genres. There are many on the market, and if you're like one friend of mine who claims to read four to five romance novels or novellas a week, you'll want to give the Amazon's subscription service a try.

You'll discover some delightfully talented writers who have self-published. With Kindle Unlimited, you can read as many as you can get your hands on.

5. Makes "browsing" of eBooks much easier and free of risk.

There are few among us who don't love to wander into a bookstore and just start browsing the shelves, opening and quickly reading a wide range of books. Some of these fit into our usual reading patterns, others are totally out of our reading comfort zone. But sometimes it's here – Bingo! – that we discover a book that captures our imagination, and we walk out the door with it.

This is exactly what Kindle Unlimited allows you to do. It gives you more flexibility in searching the "book shelves." You can easily "grab" a book, read a bit of it, and return it if it doesn't suit you. Then you move on to another potential book.

Yes, you can download a sample of just about all the ebooks on your Kindle. However, that sample is not necessarily a good indicator of what the book is about. The sample you'll receive includes the table of contents, the first several pages or the first chapter. You're quite restricted, as a matter of fact, to not only the number of pages you get to read, but also exactly what those pages are.

Browsing through a book offered through the Kindle Unlimited program gives you more freedom to check out the entire book, not just what the publisher or Amazon says you can look at.

6. Kindle Unlimited includes the downloading of audio books.

This is a definite plus for many of us. There are many individuals who ditch the regular radio or music on commutes or long drives these days and instead listen to audio books. Once the realm of only those with vision issues, audio books are gaining in popularity.

If you've been thinking about joining Kindle Unlimited, you may have already begun a list of pros and cons, advantages and disadvantages of the service. Here are just a few more of the disadvantages you can add to your list.

Disadvantages for Kindle Unlimited Readers

1. None of the major publishers is participating in the program.

If you're eager to read the next Dan Brown, James Patterson, Janet Evanovich, or J.R. Ward book through this program, you'll be disappointed. None of the major traditional publishers – usually referred to as the "Big 6" of the publishing industry or their subsidiaries or imprints is participating.

The six major publishers are:

- Hachette
- Macmillan
- Penguin Group
- HarperCollins
- Random House
- Simon & Schuster

Of course, there are still many of the smaller publishing houses participating and some of these carry books of exceptional quality. In fact, you'll find some of their authors are even on The New York Times Bestsellers List.

2. Overall, the quality of participating self-publishing books is uneven.

We've already noted it; many of the books in the program are published by the authors themselves through the Kindle Direct Publishing program. Some self-published authors have delightful books on the market. They're well written, and you wonder why a larger publisher has yet to sign them.

Quite frankly, many of the books in the Kindle Store that are self-published could certainly be improved with the aid of a series of "professional" editing sessions as traditional companies provide.

If you have little or no tolerance for poorly written books or mystery books with gigantic holes in the plot, you may find more than a few of the Kindle Unlimited choices frustrating at best.

3. **Many self-published books are priced much lower than the mainstream published books.**

Wonder why that's a disadvantage? With many of these types of books averaging around $2.99 a download (to outright purchase them) it'll take more of these books per month to make your $9.99 investment profitable. You'll need to download a minimum of at least three of these in a month.

The more expensive the books you read through KU, the better the return of investment you're receiving.

4. **Kindle Unlimited is offering no more than public libraries currently provide.**

Some critics of the program point out that every day more public libraries are allowing their patrons to download ebooks from their system without charging any monthly fee. All that's needed to "borrow" a book from a public library is a library card.

5. **Love to "own" your own book to read at your leisure.**

If you're the type of person who loves to actually own a book, then this program probably holds little promise for you. While you gain access to all of these books and have time to read them, you may be disappointed to have to return them.

Advantages, Disadvantages for Authors and Publishers

The following points are just a few reasons why, if you're an author, you may want to consider placing your books in the Kindle Unlimited service. As you read these, though, you may find additional personal reasons why you'd like your books to be available through this service.

Advantages to Publishers, Authors, and Self Publishers

1. **Exposure. Name Recognition. Invaluable Word of Mouth Sales.**

One author, who has books through traditional publishing houses as well as some self-published books, calls being in the Kindle Unlimited program, "great for discoverability." It basically consists of three intertwined concepts of exposure to a new audience, name recognition, and invaluable word of mouth sales.

She actually has included the Kindle Unlimited program as part of her marketing plan. While she acknowledges that could change at any time, right now at least, she's glad to receive the name recognition the service provides her By the way, she added, almost as an afterthought, "My self-published books are currently making more money for me than the books I have with traditional publishers."

Can anyone specifically credit the Kindle Unlimited program for that fact? Of course not, but it may be heralding a new trend in the publishing world.

When a new reader downloads you as an author, there's always the potential that he'll fall in love with your book. That means one more person knows your name and will begin to look for your books in other settings. That translates into name recognition. The next thing you know, from this one book which was downloaded as part of the Kindle Unlimited, your name and book are being talked about in ever growing reading circles.

2. **A reader only has to read 10 percent of the ebook for the author to receive full royalty on the transaction.**

Thanks to the "magic" of technology, Amazon can detect how much of a book a reader has paged through and supposedly read. If subscriber has read a minimum of 10 percent of an author's book, then Amazon will pay him or her the full royalty amount just as if the book had been bought outright.

3. **The huge audience that is opening up to you as an author.**

There's no doubt about it. Kindle Unlimited can get your name in front of one of the largest market of readers you're ever likely to find. This is especially important with the demise of so many "brick and mortar" bookstores. The days of the local bookstore are dwindling. Even national chains have closed like Borders, or are downsizing like Barnes and Noble.

While authors must do some marketing if they hope to create sales, just being listed on Amazon can help you sell books. If readers can access your books relatively risk free as with Kindle Unlimited, why not take advantage of it?

Disadvantages to Publishers, Authors, and Self-Publishers

The following facts are some of the reasons given by authors why they would steer clear of the Amazon-based service. If you're a self-publisher, you've no doubt given this option quite a bit of thought. As you make your decision, take the reasons here which resonate with you and add them to your personal list.

1. Promise to publish exclusively through Kindle Direct Publishers.

If you're an independent author or self-published, the only way you can take part in the Kindle Unlimited service is through participating in the Amazon-based Kindle Direct Publishing Select program. This means they sell their book only on the Kindle platform.

No other subscription service, especially the largest other two, Oyster and Scribd, have no such requirement.

2. Loss of control.

"The rules can change at any time." It's true, and as an independent author, there's not much you can do about it. At least for three months. When you enroll in the Kindle Direct Publishing program, you're pledging you'll keep your books with the service for a minimum of 90 days. After that period, you can withdraw your book.

In the meantime though, you have little to say should the Kindle Unlimited service "change the rules" on you.

Authors who sign with traditional publishers are often faced with parallel issues. When a publisher signs an author, especially a relatively unknown or first time author, s/he signs away many of his/her rights in exchange for their paying and marketing your book.

3. The royalties issue

Let's face it. As an author, you're on Amazon to make money. It's natural to think twice before placing your book on the web site. Amazon has been mum on what it's offering publishers and authors who books may be downloaded but not read.

Thanks to the amazing technology at the fingertips of today's authors, many of self-publishers are now making a living wage. Few authors who are with traditional publishers – even the Big 6 – can say that. Will that all change with the advent of the Kindle Unlimited membership service?

So, taking the plunge and joining Kindle Unlimited may seem like a huge gamble. Only you as a self-published author can make that decision.

Ready to take a 30-day free read?

If you are ready to try a 30-day free trial, you'll find it as easy as pie. This is especially true if you already have an Amazon account. You merely go to the home page for Kindle Unlimited. Here you'll be directed to click a button to start your free trial. If you already have an Amazon account, a Kindle device, and you've used your Kindle, you'll be automatically enrolled for free.

In a matter of literally seconds, you'll receive an email from Amazon welcoming you to your new venture. Yes, it's that easy. No forms to fill out no credit cards to register. Almost "scary easy."

If you've never bought anything from Amazon, then you'll have to create an account and supply your debit or credit card number and all the pertinent information that goes with that. The process is self-explanatory. You should have no troubles at all.

If you want to get the most out of the next 30 days, you need to plan on the next month to be a heavy reading month. Settle into a recliner, pour yourself a cup of coffee or Chai tea, and begin visualizing all the books you've always wanted to read. Then go to the Kindle Unlimited section of Amazon and see how your "dream book list" matches what Amazon has available.

Keep in mind, you have a maximum of ten books you can be reading at one time before you have to "return" one to get one.

The key to any free trial, though, is to remember to cancel it at the end of the month. Amazon makes it amazingly easy to cancel as well. Simply go back to the Kindle Unlimited homepage. Click cancel. No hassles. No Amazon employee will pop up trying to convince you to do otherwise. You won't feel badgered to stay in any way.

If you think you might want to cancel your membership at the end of a 30-day program, you may want to jot down the date that the freebie expires, or you'll find your debit or credit card charged $9.99 for a month of reading.

Wrapping it All Up

So you've decided whether to push that button your finger has been hovering over for a while. Either way, you're making the decision from a position of strength. Since you've read through this book, you have a clearer idea of whether the service suits your reading needs.

There's no doubt about it. For some readers, the Kindle Unlimited is a must-have service. For example, if you're a ravenous reader, especially in a specific genre of books, you're probably who Amazon was targeting. There are those who love romance novels, for example, who just devour them. Some individuals even read up to four or five of these a week. For them, quality isn't the issue. The act of reading is.

The same can be said for those who can't get enough of the cozy mystery genre. With Kindle Unlimited you now have literally hundreds of thousands of books to choose from. Some individuals using this service feel as if they found "book heaven."

On the other hand, if you're a more discriminating reader, then you may want to pass on the membership. You'll probably find that it doesn't include enough of the books, or the quality of books for that matter, that you normally gravitate to. You may discover that it's just one more charge on your debit or credit card every month.

Keep in mind, though, that Kindle Unlimited is only one of many subscription services on the internet today. Some of these sites are sponsored by various publishing companies. That, of course, by definition limits the books available. For example, the relatively new Crimson Romance publisher (an imprint of Adams Media) has a subscription service for the romance books it publishes.

Before making a decision regarding Kindle Unlimited, you may want to check out other similar services.

Should you take the plunge?

For authors and publishers, the issue of joining Kindle Unlimited may very well be a gamble. Being a new entity, it doesn't have any type of track record by which authors and readers alike can measure its quality. The best you can do, whether you're a reader or an author, is to review the contents of this book.

You may also want to talk to others of like mind. Do you belong to any reading forums? Can you gauge what some of your friends or cyber friends think about the program? If they've already given it a test drive, ask them if they would recommend it.

Similarly, if you're potentially thinking about self-publishing, consider consulting with other authors whose books are in the program. Ask them about their level of satisfaction with Kindle Unlimited. Gain from their experience.

Thanks to a 30-day free trial, you really risk nothing to check it out to discover if it suits your reading needs. As a self-publishing author, your commitment is three months long – 90 days. That should be enough time to give you a feel for whether it can help generate excitement, and most of all, sales for your work.

Whatever decision you make, you've made it from a position of strength.

Resources

http://www.amazon.com/gp/help/customer/display.html?nodeId=201550610

https://www.amazon.com/gp/product/B00NWRMV9G/ku?ie=UTF8&*Version*=1&*entr

http://www.cbsnews.com/news/what-you-should-know-about-kindle-unlimited/

http://www.stevescottsite.com/kindle-unlimited-thoughts

http://www.cnet.com/news/amazon-kindle-unlimited-good-for-customers-not-so-good-for-authors/

http://the-digital-reader.com/2014/11/24/kindle-unlimited-rumored-launch-brazil-early-2014/

http://the-digital-reader.com/2014/11/04/kindle-unlimited-launches-spain-italy/

http://www.stevescottsite.com/kindle-unlimited-thoughts#ixzz3RT7OFfDf

http://www.huffingtonpost.com/mark-coker/is-kindle-unlimited-bad-f_b_5615224.html

http://janefriedman.com/2014/12/02/indie-authors-kindle-unlimited/

http://contently.net/2014/08/07/stories/authors-take-advantage-kindle-unlimited/

http://boom-books.com/pros-cons-of-kindle-unlimited-vs-scribd-oyster-prime-or-playing-the-field/

www.ingramcontent.com/pod-product-compliance
Lightning Source LLC
Chambersburg PA
CBHW071203220526
45468CB00003B/1138